I STAND WITH THE SOUL OF AMERICA

A belief in the possibility of betterment, justice, and human potential.

ADDISON WITT

DEDICATION

To my beloved country, America, I stand with your soul. We are living in times of unprecedented challenges—times that echo past atrocities and remind us of the resilience required to overcome them. Our fight is on American soil, and democracy itself is at stake. It will take all freedom-loving people to resist oppression, to preserve democracy, and to reject the darkness that threatens our way of life. Now is our moment to rise, to come together, and to protect the spirit of freedom that defines us. I stand with you, America.

To my mother, Bernice; my sister, Kaduland; and my brother, Kelvin: I dedicate this book to you with boundless love and eternal gratitude.

Our journey has been long, yet together, we have met every struggle, upheld by bonds of unbreakable love and resilience. My sister, Kaduland, a true warrior, has faced health battles that would make most falter, but her spirit shines, bright and unwavering, a beacon of courage.

My mother has been her steadfast protector, a guardian ensuring Kaduland's comfort, dignity, and care. My brother, Kelvin, the quiet hero, has given of himself freely, offering strength and support, often at the expense of his own pursuits. Their sacrifices, rarely celebrated or acknowledged, are the ultimate acts of love and commitment.

Though there may be no parades or accolades for the quiet strength they have shown, this book is my tribute to them.

They are my foundation, my inspiration. In standing with them, I stand with the soul of America.

ACKNOWLEDGMENT

I want to express my deepest gratitude to my family—my mother, Bernice Robinson, my sister, Kaduland Robinson, and my brother, Kelvin Robinson. You have been my rock, my inspiration, and my unfailing support. Your resilience and sacrifices have shaped who I am and given me the strength to put my words out into the world.

To my friends and loved ones who believed in me every step of the way, I am endlessly thankful for your encouragement and support. Each of you has been a light on this journey, helping me find my voice and purpose.

To my TikTok community, where this journey of political poetry began—you hold a special place in my heart. It was with you that I shared my first poem, *Thumbs Up at Arlington,* a piece that changed my life. Through your support and engagement, I found the courage to explore deeper themes and speak with conviction. You have been my audience, my sounding board, and my inspiration.

To the political process in the United States—this 2024 campaign cycle gave me the impetus to delve into political themes, exploring the impact of policies, movements, and leaders on the lives of the American people. The experience has been a profound one, allowing me not only to offer inspiration but also to be inspired by the strength and spirit of those who engage in shaping our country's future.

To the incredible team at Amazon—thank you for your insight, your patience, and your willingness to work with me until we shaped this book into what we envisioned.

Your dedication has made this project possible, and I am grateful for your partnership.

And to you, the readers of this book, I thank you for taking this journey with me. It is my hope that these poems will inspire you, as they have inspired me, to stand with the soul of America.

CONTENTS

ABOUT THE AUTHOR

Addison Witt is an actor, educator, and writer with a deep passion for political discourse, poetry, and storytelling. Born with a love for the arts, Addison has dedicated his career to exploring the nuances of character, history, and the human spirit, whether through acting or the written word. With a rich background in the performing arts, Addison is also a seasoned acting coach, sharing his knowledge and experience with emerging talent.

In the 2024 election cycle, Addison found a new outlet for his voice on TikTok, where he began writing and sharing politically inspired poetry that resonated with thousands. His first viral piece, *Thumbs Up at Arlington,* marked the beginning of a powerful journey, connecting him with a community passionate about America's future. This book, *I Stand with the Soul of America,* is a testament to that journey and reflects Addison's commitment to speaking truthfully about the complexities of American life, unity, and hope.

Addison lives by the belief that art is a form of activism and that words have the power to inspire and ignite change. Through his work, he strives to celebrate resilience, honor diversity, and encourage meaningful dialogue.

AUTHOR'S NOTE:

REFLECTIONS ON *THE SOUL*

OF AMERICA

As I release *The Soul of America*, I find myself reflecting deeply on the journey that inspired this work. This book is not just a collection of poetry and prose; it is a heartfelt exploration of the ideals, struggles, and enduring spirit of democracy—a tribute to the people, values, and land that define us.

As an advocate of democracy, I have always cherished the opportunity to participate in the electoral process and to voice my hopes and support for leaders who reflect the vision of an inclusive and resilient nation. During the Presidential election of 2024, I supported Vice President Kamala Harris, as I believed she represented the path to preserving and strengthening our democracy. However, with the conclusion of the election and Donald Trump emerging as the victor, I recognize that my work must transcend political outcomes.

Some of the text and poems within *The Soul of America* speak to a vision rooted in the hope for different results. Yet, the heart of this book—and the ideals it upholds—remains steadfast. Democracy is not just about one election or one leader; it is a living, breathing process that belongs to us all, regardless of who holds office.

This book celebrates the soul of America not as a reflection of a single moment, but as a testament to its resilience and capacity for renewal. It honors the struggles, the voices, and the dreams that have carried this nation through its trials and triumphs. Though leaders may change, the essence of democracy—our shared commitment to a better future—endures.

As we move forward into this new chapter of our nation's story, I hope this work inspires reflection, dialogue, and a renewed dedication to the principles that bind us together. The soul of America is not confined to politics; it is found in our collective hope, our courage, and our unyielding pursuit of a more perfect union.

I STAND WITH THE SOUL OF AMERICA

In the echoes of empires that once fell
and rose again with the morning sun,
we emerge from the molten forge of progress,
each heartbeat casting sparks into the wind.

The time is no longer just "now"—
it is the pulse of eternity in this breath,
the wheel of ages spinning
in the flicker of our choices.

We stand not on mere ground,
but on the bones of old dreams,
and with every step, we stir the dust of what was,
building bridges out of ashes

and carving new paths where none existed before.
We do not rise—we bloom,
like roots cracking stone,
like shoots breaking through frost,

reaching toward the endless sky
with hands open, not clenched in fists,
but ready to weave threads of hope
through the fabric of this vast land.

No longer do we look back at the echo
of a figure once blurred in carnival glass—

distorted, yet claiming clarity.
Now, the chaos is no longer a gust;
it is the storm we must endure,
the fire rekindled, blazing through the night.
And yet, beneath the ash and roar,
we are the ember—steady, unyielding.

This is not just a reckoning;
it is the call of our collective soul.

it is a call to rise higher,
to hear the symphony of voices
in the streets, in the fields,
from the rivers to the towers of steel and glass.

We are not just Americans.
We are the restless tide, the thunder,
the hum of the cosmos beneath our feet,
citizens of a world turning its face
to the warmth of possibility,
not fractured by the past but forged anew
in the fire of compassion.

Let us leave behind the anchors of division—
the rusted chains of hatred and fear,
the weapons of a war we never wanted to fight.

We are more than red and blue;
we are the living green of fields and forests,
the golden hues of harvest,
the deep blues of oceans that cradle our shores.

It is not about rising anymore—
it is about ascending,
lifting the weight from our shoulders,
leaving behind selfishness and the politics of greed,
leaving behind the violence that scars us all.
We are not afraid of the leap,
for we are the boldest dreamers the world has ever
known.
Our future is vast,

a constellation of promises waiting to be kept,
a horizon unmeasured, waiting for our feet to cross.
In the heartbeat of this second, everything begins.
Now is the time to embrace the unspoken truth

that we are, at our core, an undivided force,
bound together not by flag, but by spirit.
We are America's breath,
rising like dawn mist over mountains,

expanding like galaxies on the edge of infinity.
This is our moment to soar.

YOU MISSED THE MOMENT

You missed the moment,
When the air was thick with hope,
When unity stretched her hand,
And family, like a warm embrace,

Pulled us all close, tight, in view.
You missed the moment,
When trust, like a gentle whisper,
Was spoken between hearts,

And dignity stood tall, unbowed,
In every voice, in every tear.
You missed the moment,
When self-respect walked proud,

Not in the shadows of doubt,
But in the full light of day,
Where every soul could see its worth.
You missed the moment,

When community, like an ancient song,
Echoed through the halls of our nation,
Calling each name, each story, each life,
To come together, to stand as one.

You missed the message,
Not for lack of words,

But for the noise within,
The clamor of judgment,

Drowning out the heart's true call.
You cried for healing,
But were blind to its gentle touch,
As it wove through the speeches,
As it rose in the music,
As it danced in the eyes of the young and old.

This was the moment,
A time for a new song,
A time for hands to join,
For voices to rise,

For a nation to breathe as one.
But you missed it,
Caught in the repetition of days long gone,
In the dark corners of second guessing,

While the light of a new dawn,
Spread its wings across the sky.
You missed the moment,
But it's not too late,

For moments like these,
They come again,
In every heart that chooses to hear.
So open your ears,

Open your heart,
Feel the pulse of a nation,
Feel the beat of a people,
Who refuse to retreat,

Who will not be denied,
Their place, their time, their right to rise.
You missed the moment,
But now you see,

That unity, family, trust, and grace,
Are the gifts we've always had,
The gifts we give,
The gifts we are.

POLITICS SHOULD NOT
CLAIM OUR SOULS

It is but a tool,
To help us navigate,
To a place of unity,
Of true love,

For self, for others,
For the nation we can be.
We stand at a crossroads,
The path behind, filled with shadows,

The path ahead, lit by our hopes.
We can choose to rebuild,
To bring this company, this country,
Together once more.

Or we can return to the crime scene,
Where greed and fear ruled the day,
Where our inner monsters roamed free.
But let us remember frost,

And the road less traveled,
The choice that made all the difference.
This is an epic decision,
Not just of politics,

But of the heart,
Of the soul.
Find your heart,
Let it lead the way,

And stand with the soul of America,
For the future we all deserve.

THE CROSSROADS OF CHOICE

I stand with the soul of America,
Where paths diverge in yellow woods,
And choices must be made in quiet,
Not by the loud, but by the good.

Joe crossed the aisles, a bridge of trust,
Kamala, with her nurturing hand,
Offers more than words can muster,
A hope to heal this fractured land.

Yet still, I hear the whispers cold,
Of wealth and privilege, blind to see,
A vote for Trump, their truth retold,
In dollars, not in unity.
They walk a path that's worn and grey,
Where shadows cast a greedy light,
And those who've less are told to stay,
To wait their turn, or face the night.

But there's a truth they do not know,
A road they've missed in their advance,
For what is wealth, if all below,
Is left to perish, left by chance?

This revelation comes with weight,

A call to lead, to rise and stand,
To guide this nation from its fate,
And not let greed take up command.

This is our vote, a step in time,
Not just for now, but for what's next.
To see ourselves in every line,
To be the better, to be the best.

For we're not just a single voice,
But reflections of a greater dream,
In which each soul has made a choice,
To cross the stream, to meet the team.

Kamala's path is different still,
A winding way through hills unknown,
Not just to follow, but to fill,
The gaps where seeds of hope are sown.
For politics should guide our way,
Not claim the heart, nor dim the soul,
But lead us through this dawning day,
To unity, to make us whole.

So stand we must, at this crossroad,
With eyes that see, with hearts that feel,
For though the past is heavy load,
The future's here, its promise real.

Let us not tread the path of fear,
Where monsters lurk, and greed is king,
But find the road less traveled here,
And let that choice be everything.

For in the end, it's not the gold,
Nor power's grasp that makes us free,
But in the love, both new and old,
That shapes our shared humanity.

So choose we must, with care and grace,
To stand with those who'd light the flame,
And walk with courage in this place,
To stand with America's name.

TO POETRY AND TO SELF

In times when shadows crowd my door,
When the world seems too heavy to bear,
I find myself in the arms of verse,
A refuge, a balm, a silent prayer.

Through the ages, across the miles,
In the heart of Beverly Hills or the quiet night,
Poetry has been my constant guide,
A beacon in the darkest fight.

When the world was masked and hearts were still,
When fear was a fog that none could see through,
I turned to the ancient words, the timeless rhymes,
Finding solace in each line, each truth anew.

In the cradle of Los Angeles dreams,
Where my craft took root and began to grow,
I found in poetry a solid ground,
A foundation that would never let go.

I served at tables, poured the wine,
In a city where stars were the lights in the night,
But it was the verses that fed my soul,
That nourished my spirit, that set me right.

For in each stanza, each meter and beat,
I saw the world with clearer eyes,

I felt the pulse of a greater love,
In every word, a new sunrise.

In moments of joy, in hours of pain,
In the turning of the nation's tide,
I sought the lines that could express,
The depths and heights I felt inside.

For poetry, my quiet friend,
You've been my voice when words fell short,
You've been my comfort, my release,
My confidant in life's long court.
You've walked with me through every stage,
From the hamlet's floors to the city's stage,
In the annals of history, the cries of now,
You've given me strength to turn the page.

And so I write this love to you,
To the art that's been my truest guide,
To the words that hold my heart's own truth,
To the lines where my spirit has always lied.

For I see now, in this revelation's light,
That poetry is not just a pastime, a craft,
It's the very thread that weaves my soul,
The steady hand that's always chaffed.

In the darkest night or brightest day,
In the laughter shared or the tear's soft fall,

Poetry is the echo of my heart,
The truest friend, the most enduring call.

So here I stand, with pen in hand,
With gratitude for the gift you've been,
To poetry, my love, my lifelong muse,
You've made me more than I've ever seen.

And as I journey on this path,
Through all the trials life may send,
I know I'll always have in you,
A faithful guide, a steadfast friend.

A RECKONING AT THE CAPITOL

We've seen dark days,
When the heart of a nation,
Built on promises stitched in stars and stripes,
Faltered under the weight of those
Who believed violence to be the answer.

January 6th will never be forgotten,
Etched in history like so many others
Where the flame of hatred,
Fueled by falsehoods,
Scorched our soil.

We remember the hands raised in violence,
The voices lifted in fury,
And the lives shaken to their core.
But we must also remember those
Who stood firm,
Who knew this land was built on valor
Not vitriol.

America, in search of its more perfect union,
Has always grappled with the weight
Of its own contradictions—
Equality promised,
But too often deferred.

17

The call to arms should never be
Against your neighbor,
Your fellow citizen,
The hands that help you build
And share this ground.
Your guns, a privilege,
Not a tool for tyranny,
And your rights, an honor,
Woven into the tapestry
Of freedom and responsibility.

No leader should summon hate,
For the spark of fear
Can burn the whole house down.

It undermines who we are,
What we've fought for,
And what we still strive to be.
In our darkest moments,
We must remember—

We do not find strength
In tearing each other apart,
But in standing together,
In confronting what divides us
With the spirit of unity.

Those who distort the truth,

Who gaslight the past,
Try to rewrite the pages
Of our history.
But we will not forget.

From the civil war to the riots of rage,
We've seen this pattern before—
Hatred disguised as righteousness,
Violence sold as the answer
To inequality's questions.

But America still stands,
A shining city on the hill,
Not because of those
Who sought to break it,
But because of those
Who raised it up.

Every attack, foreign or domestic,
Challenges our faith in this fragile union,
But each time,
We reckon with our own truth.

We are stronger when we choose justice,
Mightier when we embrace peace.
This nation,
Built on the dreams of the free,

Cannot be led by those

Who encourage destruction,
For they lack the wisdom of the past
And the vision for a future
Worthy of our struggle.

If you seek a leader,
Look not to the loudest voice,
But to the values
That have kept this land whole—

To the commitment of those
Who've come before,
Who believed in a more perfect union,
One that bends toward justice

But never breaks.
And so we remember,
We rise,
We reach again
For that beacon of light
That still shines

FREEDOM'S COST

There is an hour, uncomfortable and sharp, when the
power of the nra and goa, with their iron grips, drowns
out the cries of grieving mothers. Nagr, saf, fpc—
Their acronyms shield them like armor, but who
shields us?
Who shields our children?

We talk of rights,
Like beads strung along a rosary of freedom, but at
what price
Does the chain snap and fall?
What does it cost

To raise hope in a land
Where hope is dashed
By a bullet meant for someone else, but finds its mark
in a classroom,
In a theater,

In a park where a ball once rolled carefree?
A child with a gun
Mirrors back to us
The unspoken violence we nurse,

The sharp-edged words of our arguments,
Family feuds whispered at barbecues,
Echoing in minds too young to understand
That exaggeration

Is not an invitation to kill.

Is it too late?
Are we too far gone to change?
America is free to be,
Even if it means we are free
To bury our own.

The streets run with parades of sorrow, where flags
wave above bodies
And fireworks fall silent beneath the sound
Of rapid gunfire. A child, unhinged, becomes the
executioner of dreams.
What cost does freedom require?

Have we spent it all—
Emotionally bankrupt, politically paralyzed, spiritually
void?
Did we forget that freedom comes to collect
In the name of consequences?

From shore to shore, we whisper the names:
Colorado, florida, california, texas too. Utah,
kentucky, iowa, new york no less. North carolina,
washington, south carolina, oregon, hawaii, illinois,
massachusetts, ohio, pennsylvania, virginia, wisconsin,
nevada, connecticut, michigan, and on it goes.
Land of the free, but do we not have the right
To be free of fear
That our children

Won't make it home tonight?

When I send my kids to school, who will stand against
the cruel?
Parents arm their children
With more than love—

Bullets loaded, and still, we say, kids will be kids.
What if the cost of a gun
Came with a new law?
When you buy a weapon, you sign your name, not just
to paper, but to your child's fate.

If they pull the trigger, you pull the weight. When your
child kills my child, you pay. You serve the time. You
bear the stain.
Our children,
The future we fight to save, are handed weapons
Instead of wisdom. We say, don't get rid of them
before they're born—
But when they come,
They're left to fend for themselves.
For guns make us feel safe, until they don't.

So tell me, what is freedom's cost
When it's bought with the blood
Of the innocent?

We stand here, broken-hearted, and until we face the truth,
There will be no action, no change, no chance
For a tomorrow
That does not bleed like today.

TO MY MELANIN KIN

I remember when I was small,
And a young man knocked on our door.
He was black, like me,
And he asked my mother—

"will you come to Dr. King's rally?"
I remember her eyes,
How they softened,
How she nodded,

And I watched her dress for the march,
Head held high, ready to stand.
That was my first taste of politics,
The taste of courage,
Of a movement bigger than us,
Bigger than fear.
But today, I see something else.

I see my brothers and sisters,
Hesitant to embrace change—
A leader who reflects the strength of our mothers, our
daughters,
Those who marched with courage beside Dr. King,
Fighting for justice with nothing but hope and
determination.

Why do we shrink back
From the very prayers we whispered for generations?

I speak to you,
My brothers, my sisters,
My friends who turned to the familiar—
I understand the anger, the frustration,
The sense that this system was never built for us.

But when you align with those
Who have never carried our burdens,
What do you truly gain?
To those finding their way in politics,
I salute you.

I know you are weary,
Disillusioned by broken promises,
By a world turning on the axis of greed.
But I urge you to look again—
See that our fight is still unfolding,
That every vote cast
Is a thread in the tapestry of a dream not yet complete.

We don't seek perfection in leadership,
For perfection is a myth.
We seek those who carry the dream forward,
Who speak boldly when silence would suffice.

They rise, not because it is simple,
But because it is essential.
They are us—
And when we dismiss them,

We turn away from our own reflection.
So to my brothers, my sisters,
To my friends, and the newly awakened—
Remember the knocks on the doors of your past,

The rallies your mothers walked to,
The dreams they held for you.
Do not let their sacrifice be in vain.
We stand together,

Because divided,
We fall.

LEGACY MEDIA

What happened to the media's pride?
He called you fake, and you complied.
What happened to taking a stand,
For the people, for this land?

Once you were the voice of truth,
Now you bend with every sleuth.
Chasing clicks and viral trends,
Forgetting where your duty ends.

You once held power in your pen,
A safeguard for the rights of men.
But now you serve the highest bidder,
The line between truth and lies grows thinner.

Where's the fire, where's the fight?
The headlines now just blur the light.
You work for power, profit, spin,
While democracy dies within.

We need the press to stand upright,
To call out wrong, defend what's right.
But now you work for the machine,
Forsaking all you once had seen.

SUNDOWN TOWN

In the daylight, all looks clean,
But nightfall hides what's rarely seen.
A whispered rule, a silent frown—
Don't linger here when the sun goes down.

The streets are quiet, lined with trees,
But hate still lingers in the breeze.
A town built on fear and shame,
Where history carved another name.

No signs were posted, none to read,
But still, you'd better take your heed.
If you're black, don't dare stay late—
This town will tell you what they hate.

The sunset brings a heavy weight,
The darkness holds a quiet fate.
One misstep, one glance too long,
And suddenly, you don't belong.

The laws won't speak, the people won't shout,
But you'll know quick what it's about.
The welcome here is only skin,
And those not white are kept within.

You hear it said,
"that was the past,"

But shadows still on fences cast.
The fear that walks when dusk sets in,

Reminds us of where it's always been.
Do you feel safe when the stars are high?
Or do you glance up at the sky,
Knowing once, not long ago,

This town was built on blood's slow flow?
Sundown town, your time's expired,
But still, your gates are closed and wired.
And until those chains are fully torn,

We'll never see a world reborn.

THUMBS UP AT ARLINGTON

He stood among the stones of white,
Where heroes rest in endless night,
But in his eyes, no reverence shone,
No honor in his heart was known.

He, the man who speaks so loud,
Who wears his arrogance like a shroud,
Could not perceive the sacred ground,
Where valor, lost, is ever found.

He talks of strength, of might, of pride,
But in his soul, there's naught inside,
No understanding of the pain,
Of those who've borne the war's harsh strain.

At Arlington, where silence reigns,
He failed to feel the soldiers' chains,
That bind them to this hallowed place,
In service, in death, in honor's grace.

He stepped on graves as if they were
But stones beneath a man's cruel stir,
His thumbs raised high, as though he'd won,
A game, a match, a war undone.

But this is not his playground here,
No boxing ring, no crowd to cheer,

This is where the brave lie still,
Where sacrifice has paid the bill.

He doesn't know the meaning, true,
Of giving all, of seeing through,
A promise made to country's call,
To stand, to fight, to risk it all.
He's never faced the battle's heat,
Nor felt the drum of war's hard beat,

He speaks of power, deals, and fame,
But has no sense of duty's claim.
The military, always proud and tall,
Now whispers low, a mournful call,

"remove this man, this petty king,
Who knows not what our honor brings."
For in his reign, there's only scorn,
For those who've bled, for those who've borne,

The weight of freedom's fragile thread,
While he steps lightly on the dead.
It's time, they say, to end this farce,
This tour of failure, void and sparse,

For leadership is more than might,
It's knowing when to serve the right.
He's shown the world his shallow side,
His thumbs-up high, his lack of pride,

But history will judge him true,
As one who never really knew.
That sacrifice is not a game,
It's not a prop, it's not for fame,

It's what the brave have always known,
That freedom's cost is not their own.
So let him fade, let him depart,
With all his bluster, all his art,

For in the end, it's clear to see,
He's never grasped what it means to be.
An American, with duty's call,
To rise, to stand, to give it all,

He'll be remembered, not for might,
But for the darkness in his light.

THE POWER IN OUR HANDS

In '61, a voice so clear,
Jfk stood strong, sincere.
"ask not what your country gives,
But what you'll do, how you will live."

Yet here we stand, a shift we've seen,
Expecting one man to intervene.
A president's no king, we know,
No savior here to fix our woe.

Our neighborhoods, our streets, our towns,
It's up to us to turn things 'round.
A leader's role, they often claim,
But one alone? That's just a game.

"let's not negotiate from fear,"
But from strength, as JFK made clear.
"civility is not for show,
It's what we need to help us grow."

Politicians fan the flame,
Pointing fingers, laying blame.
They lie, divide, deflect the truth,
Ignoring facts to sway our youth.

So, let's rise up, and take our stand,
The power's still within our hands.

It's time to fire those who stall,
And hire those who hear the call.

Fire the liars, the ones who deceive,
The ones who make us all believe
That only they can fix it all—
When it's we, the people, who must stand tall.

For as jfk once said so true,
This land we love is up to you.
"here on earth, god's work's our own,"
Together we rebuild this home.

THIS HOUR IS OURS

I see in you the fight you've carried,
The weight of a world bending your back,
And still, you press forward—undaunted.
We are more than the screams reverberating in our
streets,

More than the bullets that pierce our children's futures,
More than the lies designed to suffocate truth.
This is our hour—don't you feel it?
A time when our voices refuse to ask permission,

Our songs break free, rising like dawn,
Shaking the cobwebs of apathy,
Rattling the hearts of those who thrive on division.
We are more than the blood they spill,

More than the hate they preach.
We are the pulse of democracy,
Beating in defiance,
The ones who cannot bow to tyrants,

The ones who know
There is no turning back.
They wish for an autocrat—
They crave control, a world bent by their fear.

But we hold our ground against their schemes,

Their hollow promises,
Their attempts to take apart what we've built.
We are not blind to the poison they spread—

Poisoned air, poisoned minds,
Oceans that choke while they ignore
The dying dreams.
250 years of a promise not yet kept,

A debt unpaid.
And still, we stand.
This is our hour—don't you feel it?
A time when we no longer ask,

But demand:
The truth, the justice, the sacrifice.
I see in you the fire that refuses to be snuffed out,
A flame against the darkening tide,

A refusal to let them consume
All we have fought for.
Where are you now, shining city on the hill?
Where is your light?

They would distract us with glitter and gossip,
With their noise and their shameless lies,
But we know what matters.
We know the call,

That beats in our chests,
Echoes in our streets.
We are more than their noise.
We are more than their destruction.

Of laws,
Of Values,
Of our decency,
We are America—

Flawed but unbroken.
And this is our hour.
They try to claw us back to a past
That could never truly last,

But we—
We are the future they cannot tame.
And when they choose fear,
We utter sounds of a victor's call

It pierces the wind,
It is our freedom call,
Of resistance.
Do you not hear it?

The sound of chains breaking,
The roar of a people rising
For what is right.
Do you not see it?

The faces of those before us,
Whose blood and dreams built this land,
Calling us to carry it forward, the ancestors
This is our hour—don't you feel it?

We are more than their fears,
More than their hate.
We are America, the great.
And we stand.

Now,
We stand,
Now.

STAND IN THE GAP

Democracy hangs by a thread,
Some wish it dead, others dread.
Autocrats lure with schemes and lies,
A nation at risk, where truth slowly dies.

Propaganda pours, choking our skies,
Where sea life falters, where justice cries.
Once, we stood as a beacon of light,
Now torn apart by an endless fight.

250 years, and the debt's unpaid,
Promises made, but freedom delayed.
Social programs, ripped from our hands,
Environmental dreams sinking in quicksand.

Is this the hour democracy falls?
Will we answer, or ignore the call?
The time is now—we cannot turn back,
We must rise, or face the attack.

Where is the leadership that truly matters?
Where is the sacrifice as democracy shatters?
A generation called to hold the line,
To stand in the gap, with fire divine.

The intolerant march, the corrupt thrive,
But we are America—we're still alive.

Truth, substance, commitment—it's time,
To fight for the nation, to reclaim the climb.

The headlines dazzle, the distractions swell,
But beneath the surface, there's more to tell.
Misinformation grips us every day,
While power-hungry forces plot their sway.

But to those who hear the calling deep,
Stand now, awaken from your sleep.
With fire in our eyes, and hope in our chest,
We fight for democracy—won't settle for less.

THE NATION IN TWILIGHT

Donald speaks of Haitians, with lies wrapped in fears,
"they feast on dogs and cats,
"he bellows in our ears.
But truth is distant, buried deep, hidden,

While justice is compromised, behind doors forbidden.
A court once high, now tarnished and bought,
Supreme no longer in honor, but fraught.
Justices working to clear his path,

Compromised souls, shielding him from wrath.
Assassination attempts, but who can trust?
Suspicion lingers, the plotters turn to dust.
An endless loop of a twilight zone,

Where the truth is twisted, power overthrown.
The trauma he brings spreads far and wide,
Corrupt leaders of despair stand at his side.
Look deep into the eyes of those who bow,

Their souls surrendered, no questioning now.
We must claim our soul by entering the gate,
In this parallel world, torn by the hand of fate.
Do we stay in this loop where darkness reigns,

Where loyalty's bought, and integrity wanes?
Or rise from this twilight, with courage as guide,
Reclaiming the truth that no lie can hide.
For we are the many, the power is ours,

Not his empty words or his towering towers.
We must wake from the spell before it's too late,
And forge a new path, untangled from hate.

JUSTICE, INJUSTICE

What has Donald trump revealed,
In the name of power, truth concealed?
A nation's soul, so out of tune,
A storm beneath a broken moon.

Laws for some, for others none,
What justice fades beneath the sun?
A man who cheats, who lies and steals,
And yet, his name the land reveres.

Like petulance, he struts and strides,
While many follow, lost in lies.
They mock the land they claim to love,
While traitor's hearts lie unspoken, shoved.

Against their interests, blind they vote,
The constitution sinks like a boat.
Courtly men, who swore to stand,
Bend and bow to his command.

So where is truth, where is the cost?
When virtue's gained but all is lost?
In every lie, a nation bleeds,
In every heart, a planted seed.

The price of loyalty is steep,
To follow him, the nation weeps.
Traitors to law, to fellow men,
We must find our soul again.

THE CALL

There's a call deep in my bones,
An ancient whisper that releases me from fear's cold
grip,
Quiet, yet a powerful voice unlocking hope again—
Hope for what this land could be,

For the promise made 250 years ago.
Still hanging, still unpaid—
This debt demands to be met.
It stirs within you too,

Though faint at first,
A whisper nearly lost in the noise,
In the murmur of naysayers and dog whistles,
In the distractions of a world content with looking
away.
But still, it beckons you,
Moving up your spine,
Asking— will you answer?
Or will you turn away,

Distracted by the petty,
The scornful,
Those who laugh at change,
Who shrink from progress

And dwell on mistakes long past?
This call persists—

To rise, to do something, to go higher.
The opposition is loud, but the call—

It's more than a murmur now.
It's a shout, rolling like waves crashing onto our
shores,
From mountain peaks touched by the sky
To the depth of valleys etched by time.

It shouts: act now.
There is no time to sit idle. We cannot abide book-
burners,
Those who seek to erase our rights,
To poison the halls of justice

And leave black bodies
On cold, hard streets. We cannot stand silent
As parents buy guns
For their children

To mow down other children in schoolyards.
The time for action is here,
To fight laws that leave women bleeding in alleyways,
Denied care,
While a small few dictate the rules
With no love for us at all.
This call is resounding—
No longer a whisper,

But a roar, vast and endless as the ocean,

Stretching from coast to coast,
From skyscrapers rising to meet the clouds
To towns forgotten in the heartland. We are called to
stand

Against the isms that divide us—
Racism, sexism, ageism, xenophobia, antisemitism.
We are called to recognize the moment
When leaders steer us down roads of hate. We've seen
this before—

Those who sought to cage and enslave,
To strip away dignity and humanity.
Still, the call rises, above chaos and fear.
It's bigger than you, than me.

It is the inalienable right, the freedom we are born to.
Martin heard it.
Presidents carried it. And we— we are the foot
soldiers of change,
The ring of freedom moving through time,
Never silenced, never shut out.

This village, this shining city on a hill,
Needs you.
For the greatest America to rise,
For the land to be free,

You must answer this call. Gather your heart,
Your mind,

Your spirit.
Bring all that you possess,

For this fight requires it. Answer this call with
everything you have. We are not just seeking a
president— we are demanding a debt paid,
Demanding the future we were promised.
This is the time.

This is the call.

CONSPIRACY IS THE THING

The conspiracy
Is the thing—
Conditioned into us
Like a slow drip,

An opportunity seized
By the self-indulgent,
The irresponsible,
The avaricious.

They dress it up in truth,
A deceit wrapped in certainty,
As though we can't see
With our own eyes

Or hear our own voices. Some will believe
Anything shouted long enough—
Salacious, deranged,
Madness becomes momentum,

Propelled by the muttering
That slither into conversations,
That morph into plans,
Covert and twisted. And truth?

Where does it lie now?
A court divided,

Congress bickering in the shadow,
Even faith has lost its grip

On conviction once held tightly. Convictions—
Are they part of the conspiracy, too?
Now, conspiracy is a guide,
Like a new creed,

Democrat, republican,
Faith-based, alt-right, extreme. We live in a web of
falsehoods
Turned nightmare,
Where dreams once stood. When did this become

The thing we cling to?
It unravels what we know. And look at the prophets of
lies,
Those who carry falsehoods,
Wrapped in plausible deniability.

They deliver deceit
With a polished tongue,
But we see it,
We hear it,

We feel it. So why do the networks indulge?
Greed?
Or the conglomerates
Pulling their strings?

They package the venom
In "what ifs,"
In "could it be's,"
Injecting fear into the airwaves. America,

Look at yourself. What once stood self-assured
Now crumbles under conspiracies,
Their weight too heavy to bear.
They crawl from the chaos,

Those who carry the lies,
Bellies dragging across the dirt,
So low there's no depth
They haven't touched.

Injecting dis-ease into minds—
And beware—
They come for more,
They come for your children,

They come for your trust.
Lost,
Swirling in the storm
Of deceit,

And here we are—
A people grasping for stability,
Clinging to promises wrapped in slogans,
Trump kindles their hopes,

Shielded by claims of "fighting for you."

But it's a facade,
Always for himself,
Surrounded by a circle steeped in the same duplicity.
Society—can you see through this?

Are we lost entirely?
No, not yet.
That quiet truth inside you,
It still breathes—waiting to be heard.
Reach for it,
Fight for it. Don't let go
Of truth,
Of yourself,

Of the future.

THE SUMMONS

In the season of the great pandemic,
The changing of ages, the veil lifted—
Revelation comes in orations and truths,
Of what was, what we believed,

And what we now see so clear.
The truth lies within you,
Stirring beneath your skin,
Its outer expression—

A mirror to your emotions,
A dance of feelings, alive, raw, and real.
Each of us is called—
To serve our purpose to completion,

To walk the path of our soul's design.
We are not merely fleeting,
But the infinite spark of all there is,
Known and unknown, forever evolving.

We are creation's breath,
The pulse of every world, every star,
Across dimensions unseen,
Through portals of wormholes and time,

We are the truth embodied,
The legacy of the ages.

Every belief has brought us here,
To this everlasting place.

Ever-turning, ever-rotating,
We evolve into more than what was,
An eternal expression of the all.
And in your summons to be here, now,
You are gifted with two powers:

Chaos and love.
Through these twin forces,
You wield the energies of the universe,
Bending them to your will.

Chaos—wild, unbridled,
The fire beneath creation.
Love—the balm, the guide,
Soft yet unbreakable.

Both live within you,
Entwined in the dance of your heart.
How you wield them is your truth,
The mark you leave upon this world.

Will you expand?
Or will you contract?
The choice is yours to make,
And the consequence,

Yours to hold.
In the universe, these forces are known—
Creation and discipline.
Chaos fuels creation,

As emotion does imagination.
You are here, now,
To carve your legacy,
With love and chaos as your tools.

What you build with them,
Will be remembered.
The choice is yours,
The time is now.

WE ARE NOT GOING BACK

Dread no more, for today dawns with hope anew,
A different light, a promise we must see through.
We are the answer, the ones we've long sought,
In our hands lies the change, the battles to be fought.

Do something, they said—so we rise,
With a fierce resolve, with fire in our eyes.
For we are ready, the story is ours to tell,
To lift the weary, to break the final shell.

We are not going back, we won't retreat,
From the path we've carved with every heartbeat.
For civil rights, for love that knows no bounds,
For every voice that in this nation resounds.

Mind your own damn business, they said with pride,
In the choices of others, you need not decide.
For freedom means living as true as we can,
Each woman, each man, following their plan.

We stand with courage, unwavering, bold,
For justice, for freedom, for truths untold.
No rollback of rights, no return to chains,
We push forward through the storms and rains.

Reproductive rights, a woman's own choice,
Her body, her life, her will, her voice.
We refuse the darkness that seeks to confine,
We march onward, to protect what is mine.

In the face of the fires, the earth's growing plea,
We fight for the land, for the sky, for the sea.
No backward step, no retreat to the past,
For the future is green, and it's coming fast.

Healthcare for all, a right, not a gift,
We push for a system that doesn't let us drift.
From the sick, the poor, the broken and frail,
We build a nation where all can prevail.

Economic justice, the worker's due,
A fairer share for me, for you.
No more favor for the wealthy's gain,
We rise for the many, we break every chain.

When we fight, we win—this truth we hold dear,
Our power, our voices, they conquer fear.
Together we stand, together we strive,
For a nation that thrives, where all can survive.

We are not going back, this is our stand,
For democracy's light, for this precious land.
Against those who would dim the rights we hold dear,
We fight, we protect, without falter, without fear.

Not one step back, only forward we go,
For a brighter tomorrow, with justice in tow.
So dread no more, let hope guide our way,
For today we stand firm, come what may.

We are not going back, this is our creed,
To sow the seeds of progress, to let them succeed.
In the hearts of the many, in the hands of the few,
We carry this promise, we make it true.
For we are not going back, no, we rise,
With strength, with hope, with unclouded eyes.

KNOW FOR YOURSELF

Some say, they didn't teach us this in school,
As if the fault lies in the lessons, gone
And passed, like leaves that drift to pools
Unnoticed, in the forest where we've drawn

Our maps and pathways, set in youthful days,
But wandered off, forgetting all the ways.
For in those halls, we sat with heads bent low,
Our thoughts on other things, our minds elsewhere,

While truths were taught, but we were slow
To see the value in the knowledge there.
Now, older, wiser—or so we claim—
We find we've missed the point of the game.

The world we face is not the same we knew,
And yet, we walk with eyes half-closed,
Believing stories that are only partway true,
Forgetting all the things we never chose

To learn, to know, to seek with open mind—
The truths we left, unclaimed, behind.
Oh, to know for oneself, to dig and find
The roots that lie beneath the soil,

To break the ground, to use the mind,

And plant the seeds of honest toil.
For knowledge comes to those who seek,
Not to the idle, nor the weak.

The times have changed, and so must we,
If we're to walk the paths unknown,
Through woods that bend and twist and free
The doubts that in our hearts have grown.

For truth is not the easy path,
But one that cuts through undergrowth and wrath.
So let us not be quick to share
The words we've heard but not yet weighed,

For in the rush, we often spare
The facts that must be carefully laid.
Know for yourself, before you speak,
For silence is a burden, but truth is not meek.

Whether it's the turning of the leaves,
Or the frost that settles on the ground,
Whether it's the wind that grieves
Or the peace that in the woods is found,

We must learn to see with clear intent,
And know the worth of what is meant.
For in the knowing, we find our way,
Through forests dark and fields of light,

And in the end, when comes the day,
We'll stand in knowledge, tall and bright.
So know for yourself, and do not fall
To ignorance—hear the higher call.

Speak with the wisdom the world requires,
And let your words be firm, yet kind,
For in the truth, there's light that inspires,
And in that light, we are not blind.

So walk the path, and do not sway,
For truth will guide us, come what may.

THE DAWN OF OUR
BECOMING

A bridge, a torch, a road,
Symbols of our journey and struggle,
Mark the passage of time and trials,
Where our ancestors once stood,

Where we now stand, between what was and what
shall be.
The sounds of their footsteps,
Etched in the stone of this earth,
Remind us of the paths worn by sacrifice,

The fields tilled by hands long gone,
Leaving traces of hope and melancholy,
In the dust of forgotten ages. But today, the bridge
speaks to us, firmly, with resolve,
Come, you may cross over into the unknown,
But seek no shelter in your fears,
For i will not carry the weight of your doubt. You,
forged in the crucible of change,
Have dwelled too long in the shadows of the past,

Have bowed too often to the chains of tradition,
Your voices muffled by the weight of history.
The bridge speaks to us today, you may walk upon me,
But do not turn your gaze backward. Across the vast
expanse of our nation,

The torch burns bright, a flame unyielding,
It says come, be warmed by my light.
Each of you a bearer of legacy,
Unique in your heritage, yet bound together,

By the shared burden of progress and the promise of
tomorrow. Your battles for justice, for truth,
Have scarred the land, but also healed it,
Leaving trails of resilience upon my soul,

And declarations of freedom in the wind. Yet, today i
call you to my light,
If you will carry peace in your heart. Come,
Clad in hope, and i will light the way,
As the creator intended when i was first ignited,

When i and the bridge and the road were one. Before
fear traced lines upon your brow,
And you forgot the power within you.
The torch burns and beckons on.

There is a deep yearning to respond,
To the guiding light of the torch and the steady path of
the bridge. So say the farmer, the doctor, the artist,
The teacher, the soldier, the student,

The believer, the skeptic, the dreamer,
The wanderer, the builder, the healer.
They all hear the call of the road.

They hear the ancient and future voices

Speaking to humankind today. Come, walk with me,
upon the road. Plant your feet upon this path.
Each of you, descendant of those who came before,
Has been chosen for this moment. You, who gave me
my first steps, you

Pioneers, trailblazers, visionaries, who
Carved your names in the annals of time, then
Handed me the torch of your dreams—
To light the way for others seeking truth,

Hungering for justice. You, the worker, the scholar,
the leader,
The artist, the seeker, arriving with hope,
Praying for a new dawn. Here, root yourselves upon
this road.
I am that road laid by the hands of the brave,

Which will not be broken.
I, the bridge, i the torch, i the road
I am yours—your inheritance has been granted.
Lift up your spirits, you have a great need

For this new morning dawning for you. History,
despite its burdens,
Cannot be unwritten, but if faced
With courage, can be the foundation of tomorrow.
Lift up your eyes upon

This day breaking for you. Give birth again
To the vision. Women, children, men,
Shape it with your hands,
Mold it with your dreams.

Lift up your hearts,
Each new moment holds new possibilities
For new beginnings. Do not be bound forever
By fear, fastened eternally

To the weight of the past.
The horizon stretches before us,
Offering space to take new steps of change. Here, in
the dawn of this new day
You may have the courage

To look up and out and upon me, the
Bridge, the torch, the road, your nation. No less to the
weary than the hopeful. No less to you now than those
who came before. Here on the pulse of this new
morning

You may have the grace to look up and out
And into your sister's eyes, and into
Your brother's face, your country
And say with conviction,

With hope,
Here, we are,
Here.

THE PATH WE WALK

It begins with a sunrise, a quiet knowing—
America stirs, the ground below glowing.
Not with fires of old, but with something new,
A vision of what we could be, shining through.

We've stood here before, on this precipice steep,
Dreaming of heights, though the climb feels deep.
But now we rise again, hands calloused and strong,
To correct the course, where we've wandered wrong.

You see, I've known the power of division's seed,
Watched as fear turned into bitter creed.
In towns and cities, where people were torn,
We forgot what it meant to be one, to be reborn.

A Shift in Leadership
The time is now—no more delay,
We stand at the dawn of a brand new day.
I see in you the strength of heart,
A people who know how to rise and start.
The People's Responsibility
We are the leaders we've waited for,
The ones who must walk through this door.
No one man or woman can heal this place,
It's in our unity, our collective grace.

We must be the hands that rebuild,

The hearts that heal, the dreams fulfilled.
No longer can we wait for someone to save,
It's us—it's us who must be brave.

We are more than our wounds and strife,
We are the song that sings of life.
The song I sing is of hope reborn,
A nation renewed, not tattered and worn.
A New America
I see in you a light, a spark,
A future that rises from the dark.
America, the land of heart and grit,
Where we're not afraid to take the hit.

The time is now, the choice is clear—
Do we rise together, or live in fear?
We must claim our soul, our better part,
And lead this nation with a united heart.
The Future We Hold
I speak not just from the head, but the heart inside,
From the struggles we've shared, the battles we've
tried.

But in this new dawn, let us take the chance,
To build a nation, where we all can dance.
We are more than the hate that divides,
Stronger than the fear that hides.

The song I sing is of freedom's call,
For when I win, we all stand tall.
The light is here, the path is clear—
Together we rise, together we steer.

AMERICA IN THE MIRROR

This is the moment—a nation, a face,
Once bold, once bright, now caught in grace,
And shadow. The world peers in close,
Watching, wondering, holding hope.

For years we stood as freedom's guard,
Our shores safe harbors, broad and starred with flags
waving.
We fought for others, held democracy's flame,

Now that torch flickers, whispering our name.
America, woven by all,
Yet torn at the seams where shadows fall.

Listen to the voices, each claiming right,
Some rage in darkness, some sing of light.
The world wonders, uncertain, still:
Is the promise alive? Does the heart beat still?

What of the dream, the city on the hill?
Will the nation of freedom, the land of the brave and
free,
Let fear reign sovereign and anger enslave?

For here on this soil lies a history vast,
Of voices raised high, of courage steadfast.
Yet now we are tested, once more in the fire—
Shall we rise anew, or will we let hope expire?

In this silence, the world holds its breath, waiting still,
Wondering, watching—will you bend or build?
Each word, each vote, each voice a call,
A choice for freedom, for one, for all.

So here we stand, at history's edge,
With hope and fear as our solemn pledge.
With hearts joined, we face the choice:
To raise a fist, or lift our voice.

THE CLARENCE THOMAS LEGACY

In July '91, a giant stepped down,
Thurgood Marshall, with a civil rights crown.
His seat now empty, a legacy vast,
In walked Clarence Thomas, conservative, steadfast.

A nominee young, just 43,
With a record that spoke of conservatism's plea.
From the eeoc to the court of appeals,
His path to the bench had swift appeal.

But then came a storm, as Anita Hill spoke,
Of harassment, of wrongs that the silence broke.
In a nation divided, her voice was clear,
Yet, in those chambers, doubt and fear.
Joe Biden, the chair, with a role so great,
Faced the task to decide Thomas's fate.
He questioned and probed, yet critics still say,
He limited voices, kept witnesses at bay.

The vote was tight, 52 to 48,
A decision that sealed Thomas's fate.
Biden opposed, but the gavel came down,
And Clarence Thomas wore the justice's gown.

But the scars of that fight, they linger and stay,

In decisions he's made, but it's the telltale who say,
A vendetta perhaps, against those who opposed,
A bench now shaped by the bitterness exposed.

The legacy deep, from that fateful day,
Changed how nominations would play.
Sexual harassment, a spotlight so bright,
Changed the discourse, brought truth to light.

The hearings a mirror, to America's face,
Revealing the struggles, the wounds to embrace.
In this chapter of history, contentious, profound,
The story of justice, where reechoes resound.

THE FUTURE WE HOLD

I speak not of endings but of what begins,
Of mornings forged from yesterday's sins.
The struggles we've borne, the battles we've faced,
Have carved us a path no hatred can erase.

In the quiet of dawn, there's a steadying gate,
A call to rebuild, to heal and create.
We hold in our hands the tools of our fate,
To shape what's ahead—it's never too late.

For we are Americans, a tapestry sewn,
By the lives we've lived, by the seeds we've sown.
Yet the heart of this land bears scars to confront,
Truths to unravel, and wounds to affront.

Let's steady our course, let's answer the call,
To face what we've hidden, to rebuild it all.
Not bound by divisions, nor shackled by fear,
But boundless in hope, our purpose made clear.

The future is ours, in the work we embrace,
In the hands we join, in the truths we face.
Together we rise, together we fight,
For a land renewed, where we build what's right.

A FAMILY OF MANY LANDS

From central Europe, roots began,
Fred trump, a German man.
His father crossed the ocean wide,
From Bavaria's fields to New York's stride.

Three wives with stories of their own,
From different lands, their seeds were sown.
Ivana from Czech's eastern lands,
In Zlín, her life first took its stand.

Marla's roots, in Georgia's clay,
An American, from the USA.
Then Melania, from Slovenia's shore,
Her eastern roots would join the lore.

Children born with mixed descent,
A blend of places where hearts were sent.
German, Scottish, czech, and more,
A melting pot at family's core.

Donald Jr., Ivanka too,
And Eric, Czech and German grew.
Tiffany, with Georgian pride,
And Barron, Slovenian ties beside.

From central Europe, eastern air,
To southern soil, their stories share.
A family tree with roots so wide,
In many lands, their hearts reside.

A TALE OF SHIFTING LOYALTIES

In days gone by, the republican hand,
Freed the chains, gave rights to stand.
In post-war times, they held the fight,
For freedom's cause, for justice's light.

But as the years rolled gently on,
The party's focus shifted, drawn
To business, wealth, a different tune,
And with it, hearts began to swoon.

In southern fields, where democrats lay,
Segregation ruled the day.
Yet whispers of change began to swell,
With Roosevelt's new deal, they rang the bell.
The 1930s brought a storm,
A promise made to those forlorn.
Though flawed in ways, the new deal's grace,
Brought African Americans to a new embrace.

The civil rights, a battle fought,
By democrats who bravely sought
To end the wrongs, to break the chains,
With laws that resounded through the plains.

The acts of '64 and '65,
Brought hope and justice, kept alive.
With Kennedy, with Johnson's pen,
They won the hearts of many men.

But in the south, a shift began,
A strategy drawn by clever hands.
White voters turned to the GOP,
While black Americans stood with the d.

Economic dreams, social care,
The democrats' touch was everywhere.
Justice, health, and welfare's call,
To African Americans, they gave their all.

Modern times brought clearer lines,
On race, injustice, changing signs.
The democrats stood firm and strong,
Their values where black hearts belong.

Candidates with skin like night,
With voices strong, they fought the fight.
For justice, rights, and all that's fair,
The democratic banner's in the air.

And so, the story, long and deep,
Explains the trust they choose to keep.
For policies and justice true,
The democratic heart they knew.

A tale of past and present days,
Where loyalty and history stay.
In justice, hope, and equal stand,
They rise united, hand in hand.

THE MOMENT WE MAKE

We gather in the shadow of history,
A future on the cusp, waiting to be seen.
Joy and optimism, where hope used to whisper,
Now shout in the streets, loud, and clean.
Our vote is our voice, the fight is clear,
We march with courage, not with fear.

This moment we hold, as fragile as glass,
A time to unite, to shatter the past.
For values are not just words we say,
They're the compass that guides us day by day.

We fight not against, but for what's right,
For children, for freedom, for futures bright.
When we know better, we do, we rise,
With justice, with dignity, under open skies.

So stand with me, in this land we create,
Each step, each voice, can shift the weight.
When history calls, what will you say?
That we stood together, and made today.

THE GRIFTED LAND

America, what story are you trying to tell? You sing about the most desirable democracy, paint yourself as the world's beacon, but now the cracks in your reflection are showing.

Donald Trump—your latest chapter, a figure whose clumsy hands tried to pull the strings of power, to tear down the truth of a free election. Al Gore stepped aside when the court took his turn, Hillary let go when the vote didn't play her way. But Trump? His grip tightens in the face of defeat. He thinks he can twist time backward, a conman wanting a kingdom built on lies.
Why, America, do so many follow paths already fractured,
Ignoring the cracks beneath their feet?
Do you embrace the illusions spun so skillfully,
The promises that echo but never solidify?
Is this the freedom your forebears envisioned,
The sacrifice they bore,
A legacy exchanged for fleeting words,
Words that falter when pressed against the weight of truth?
Violence, you welcomed it long ago: It's in your classrooms, homes, churches— it's in your very streets. A land where guns talk louder than laws, where hands that should nurture hold knives instead. Your flag waves over a battlefield of your own making.

America, this is your reflection now: violence not just
with fists but with words, with ballots, with unchecked
greed. And you bow to a man who laughs as you fall.

Can't you see? Your dream is teetering, the promises
of freedom wrapped in chains, pulled by those who
seek not your liberation, but their dominion.

Trump condones it. He breathes it in. And you,
America, what do you inhale? A poison long spread,
now infecting the very bones of a nation once admired.

Wake up, America. This isn't about politics—it's
about your soul. You hold the brush that paints your
future. What will you create?

HUMBLE, YOU SAY

Once, you told me to be seen, not heard.
But now I break through, no longer unsure.
You speak of strength in the quiet,
But my strength is the noise I make—
The choices that carve my path.
You call me back, back to the kitchen,
Back to the bedroom, where you feel safe.
You are the man, the lord,
The one I'm meant to follow.
But I've been mother to nations,
Portal to worlds unknown.
Humility, you say, makes me whole.
Makes me kind, makes me less.
You want humility to fit into your box,
To make space for your throne.
But humility is not my drive,
Nor my definition of grace.
Wisdom supersedes it,
And power walks hand-in-hand with kindness.
Too much humility is too little respect.
And I know my worth.
Humility may be a nod, a smile,
But it's not my limit.
My jaw dropped the day I realized
Humility was no longer my cage.
Now, I'm bold. I speak with hair flying,
No longer weighed down by the chains of 'quiet.'

Kamala spoke, and we listened.
The world shook,
Our voices freed,
Boldness no longer a sin.
This is our strength, our truth,
And we stand—not humble,
But powerful.

RISE

In the quiet before dawn,
Rise.
Shoulders back,
Fire in your eyes—
Rise.

Your voice roars,
Your fury ignites.
At last,
You are heard.

Shake off the chains,
Minds locked tight,
A terrible waste.
The right to defend?
Yours by birth.

But the climb is steep,
Trials test your worth.
You ask,
"Where were they?"
"What did they do?"

You say promises
Failed you,
Kicked you out of homes,
Left you out of the fight.
Others soared—
You stayed behind.
But you could have stood,

Taken the power,
Lifted your own.

Now you stand with questions,
Anger in masse.
But this,
Is a call for unity,
Rise.
Unify.

Our ancestors bled,
Fought for a dream,
Clear and undeterred.
Not for division,
Not for hate.
We are vast.
Our legacy,
Rich with giants.
Builders.
Creators.
Minds ablaze.

We rise
from this.
We must amaze.
The climb is tough,
The path steep,
But closer than ever,
We touch the sky.
When crawling feels
Like the only way,
Remember,

You are here.
You made it today.

So take our hands.
We reach out now.
This is where you begin.
This is your stand.
Step into the light,
Or fall on the shore.
Blame no more.

ARLINGTON

It's quiet here, yet alive with song—
a place of tribute and reverence, yes,
but also one of celebration:
God Bless America,
The Battle Hymn of the Republic,
filling the spaces between names,
lifting each stone, each story, each life.

Green hills roll like waves,
marked by crosses and stars,
names etched deep into stone—
whispering, remember me.
And we do—
we remember.

Today, flags pulse in the breeze,
a heartbeat for the fallen—
soldiers, mothers, fathers, sons,
and daughters who gave and went.
Silent salutes, standing guard,
from those who never left their posts.
An aged President, gray with time,
stands at the edge,
salutes to sky, to earth, to memory—
hands steady, voice a prayer,
an invocation:
Let us be worthy.

He recites names like chapters—
Korea, Iraq, Afghanistan,
Normandy, Vietnam,
each a story unfinished,
a promise that endures,
and the never-forgets.

We, the living,
stand here, shoulder to shoulder,
at the crossroads of then and now,
holding tight to the truth
that still marches on—
roots beneath these hills,
stars in endless rows.

In this sacred earth,
they rest with quiet honor—
oath-takers, front-liners,
those who believed in something greater,
those who gave until there was nothing left to give.

Look across the stones, the green,
the weight of names, the weight of years—
this is more than one story,
more than one voice.
On this ground, we remember, together,
for what was given, for what remains.

Today, we salute you—
the lives given for freedom's sake,
the legacy of valor that stands like stone,
through every age, every season.

So let this ground hold sacred what we cannot forget.
And let us carry forward
what it means to stand united,
for all that is true, for all that is free.

This, the heartbeat of Arlington—
the song of those who believed
and became part of something eternal.

Ultimately, the soul of America is most palpably found in its people. It's in the resilience of the farmers and laborers, the creativity of artists, the brilliance of scholars and inventors, and the unyielding spirit of those who advocate for justice. The soul of America is a complex, living force—a collective conscience carried forward by generations. Even when the soul feels wounded, it's also capable of incredible healing, as countless communities work tirelessly to build a more just and compassionate society.

Sir Addison Witt

Made in the USA
Monee, IL
14 February 2025

12294197R00059